50 Mastering the Basics Recipes

By: Kelly Johnson

Table of Contents

- Classic Scrambled Eggs
- Perfect Boiled Eggs
- Homemade Pancakes
- French Toast
- Grilled Cheese Sandwich
- Baked Chicken Breast
- Roasted Vegetables
- Spaghetti with Marinara Sauce
- Mashed Potatoes
- Homemade Pizza Dough
- Chicken Stock
- Beef Stock
- Rice Pilaf
- Stir-Fried Vegetables
- Caesar Salad
- Roasted Garlic
- Simple Vinaigrette

- Omelette
- Baked Potatoes
- Tomato Soup
- Chicken Salad
- Basic Risotto
- Sautéed Shrimp
- Simple Beef Stir-Fry
- Roasted Chicken
- Creamed Spinach
- Perfectly Cooked Quinoa
- Garlic Butter Sauce
- Homemade Granola
- Potato Salad
- Grilled Chicken Thighs
- Roasted Sweet Potatoes
- Tofu Stir-Fry
- Boiled Corn on the Cob
- Classic Beef Burger
- Baked Salmon

- Roasted Carrots
- Simple Fried Rice
- Vegetable Soup
- Basic Guacamole
- Perfectly Cooked Risotto
- Pan-Seared Steak
- Crispy Roasted Chicken Wings
- Cabbage Slaw
- Fluffy Biscuits
- Homemade Croutons
- Simple Tomato Sauce
- Grilled Vegetables
- Baked Mac and Cheese
- Classic Meatloaf

Classic Scrambled Eggs

Ingredients:

- 4 large eggs
- 1/4 cup milk or cream
- Salt & pepper, to taste
- 1 tbsp butter or oil

Instructions:

1. Whisk eggs, milk, salt, and pepper together in a bowl.
2. Heat a non-stick skillet over medium-low heat and melt butter.
3. Pour in the egg mixture. Stir gently with a spatula, moving eggs from the edges to the center.
4. Continue cooking, stirring occasionally, until eggs are soft and slightly runny (they will continue cooking off the heat).
5. Serve immediately.

Perfect Boiled Eggs

Ingredients:

- Eggs (as many as you like)
- Water

Instructions:

1. Place eggs in a saucepan and cover with cold water by about 1 inch.
2. Bring to a boil over high heat.
3. Once boiling, reduce the heat to low and cover the pan.
4. For soft-boiled eggs, cook for 4–5 minutes. For hard-boiled eggs, cook for 9–12 minutes.
5. Transfer eggs to a bowl of ice water to cool for 5 minutes before peeling.

Homemade Pancakes

Ingredients:

- 1 1/2 cups all-purpose flour
- 3 1/2 tsp baking powder
- 1 tbsp sugar
- 1/2 tsp salt
- 1 1/4 cups milk
- 1 egg
- 3 tbsp melted butter

Instructions:

1. In a bowl, whisk together flour, baking powder, sugar, and salt.
2. In another bowl, whisk together milk, egg, and melted butter.
3. Pour wet ingredients into dry ingredients and stir just until combined (lumps are okay).
4. Heat a griddle or pan over medium heat and grease with butter or oil.
5. Pour 1/4 cup batter onto the griddle. Cook until bubbles form on the surface, then flip and cook for 1-2 more minutes.
6. Serve warm with syrup or toppings of choice.

French Toast

Ingredients:

- 2 eggs
- 1/2 cup milk
- 1 tsp vanilla extract
- 1/2 tsp cinnamon (optional)
- 4 slices bread (preferably slightly stale)
- 1 tbsp butter
- Powdered sugar, syrup, or toppings

Instructions:

1. In a bowl, whisk together eggs, milk, vanilla, and cinnamon.
2. Heat a pan over medium heat and melt butter.
3. Dip each slice of bread into the egg mixture, ensuring both sides are coated.
4. Cook in the pan for 2-3 minutes per side, until golden brown.
5. Serve with powdered sugar, syrup, or your favorite toppings.

Grilled Cheese Sandwich

Ingredients:

- 2 slices of bread
- 2 tbsp butter
- 2 slices cheese (American, cheddar, or your choice)

Instructions:

1. Heat a pan over medium heat.
2. Butter one side of each slice of bread.
3. Place one slice of bread, butter side down, in the pan and add the cheese.
4. Top with the second slice of bread, butter side up.
5. Grill for 2-3 minutes per side, until the bread is golden brown and the cheese is melted.
6. Serve warm.

Baked Chicken Breast

Ingredients:

- 2 boneless, skinless chicken breasts
- 1 tbsp olive oil
- Salt & pepper, to taste
- Optional: garlic powder, paprika, lemon juice, herbs

Instructions:

1. Preheat the oven to 375°F (190°C).
2. Rub chicken breasts with olive oil and season with salt, pepper, and any additional seasonings.
3. Place chicken on a baking sheet lined with parchment paper.
4. Bake for 20-25 minutes, until the internal temperature reaches 165°F (74°C).
5. Let rest for 5 minutes before slicing.

Roasted Vegetables

Ingredients:

- 4 cups mixed vegetables (carrots, bell peppers, zucchini, etc.), chopped
- 2 tbsp olive oil
- 1 tsp dried thyme or rosemary
- Salt & pepper

Instructions:

1. Preheat the oven to 400°F (200°C).
2. Toss vegetables with olive oil, herbs, salt, and pepper.
3. Spread on a baking sheet in a single layer.
4. Roast for 20-25 minutes, flipping halfway through, until tender and golden.
5. Serve warm.

Spaghetti with Marinara Sauce

Ingredients:

- 8 oz spaghetti
- 1 tbsp olive oil
- 2 cloves garlic, minced
- 1 (24 oz) jar marinara sauce
- Salt & pepper, to taste
- Fresh basil or parsley (optional)

Instructions:

1. Cook spaghetti according to package instructions.
2. While pasta cooks, heat olive oil in a pan over medium heat.
3. Add garlic and cook for 1 minute, then add marinara sauce and simmer for 5 minutes.
4. Drain spaghetti and toss with sauce. Serve with fresh herbs, if desired.

Mashed Potatoes

Ingredients:

- 2 lbs potatoes, peeled and chopped
- 1/2 cup milk or cream
- 4 tbsp butter
- Salt & pepper

Instructions:

1. Boil potatoes in salted water for 15–20 minutes until fork-tender.
2. Drain potatoes and return to the pot.
3. Add butter, milk, salt, and pepper. Mash until smooth.
4. Serve warm.

Homemade Pizza Dough

Ingredients:

- 2 1/4 tsp active dry yeast
- 1 1/2 cups warm water
- 3 1/2 cups all-purpose flour
- 2 tbsp olive oil
- 1 tsp salt
- 1 tsp sugar

Instructions:

1. Dissolve yeast and sugar in warm water. Let sit for 5 minutes until bubbly.
2. In a large bowl, combine flour and salt. Add yeast mixture and olive oil.
3. Knead the dough on a floured surface for 5-7 minutes, until smooth.
4. Place dough in an oiled bowl, cover, and let rise for 1 hour.
5. Punch down dough and roll out to desired size. Top with sauce and toppings.

Chicken Stock

Ingredients:

- 1 whole chicken or 2-3 chicken breasts with bones
- 1 onion, quartered
- 2 carrots, chopped
- 2 celery stalks, chopped
- 3 cloves garlic, smashed
- 10 cups water
- 1 tsp salt, 1/2 tsp pepper
- 1 bay leaf, 2 sprigs thyme

Instructions:

1. Place all ingredients in a large stockpot and cover with water.
2. Bring to a boil, then reduce heat and simmer for 2–3 hours.
3. Skim off any foam that rises to the surface.
4. Strain the stock and discard the solids. Store in the refrigerator or freeze for later use.

Beef Stock

Ingredients:

- 2 lbs beef bones (preferably with some meat on them)
- 1 onion, quartered
- 2 carrots, chopped
- 2 celery stalks, chopped
- 4 cloves garlic, smashed
- 1-2 bay leaves
- 6-8 cups water
- 1 tsp salt
- 1/2 tsp pepper
- 1 tsp dried thyme (optional)

Instructions:

1. Preheat the oven to 400°F (200°C). Place beef bones on a baking sheet and roast for 30-40 minutes until browned.
2. In a large pot, add the roasted bones, onion, carrots, celery, garlic, and herbs.
3. Add water to the pot and bring to a boil.
4. Reduce heat and simmer uncovered for 3–4 hours, skimming off any foam that rises to the surface.
5. Strain the stock through a fine-mesh sieve and discard the solids.

6. Let the stock cool, then refrigerate or freeze for later use.

Rice Pilaf

Ingredients:

- 1 cup long-grain white rice
- 2 tbsp butter or olive oil
- 1 small onion, finely chopped
- 2 cups chicken or vegetable broth
- 1/2 tsp salt
- 1/4 tsp pepper
- 1/4 cup toasted almonds (optional)

Instructions:

1. In a medium saucepan, heat the butter or olive oil over medium heat.
2. Add the onion and cook for 2-3 minutes, until softened.
3. Stir in the rice and cook for another 2-3 minutes, allowing the rice to lightly toast.
4. Add the broth, salt, and pepper, and bring to a boil.
5. Reduce the heat to low, cover, and simmer for 15-18 minutes, until the rice is cooked and the liquid is absorbed.
6. Fluff the rice with a fork and stir in toasted almonds (if desired) before serving.

Stir-Fried Vegetables

Ingredients:

- 2 cups mixed vegetables (broccoli, bell peppers, carrots, snap peas, etc.)
- 2 tbsp vegetable oil
- 2 tbsp soy sauce
- 1 tbsp oyster sauce (optional)
- 1 clove garlic, minced
- 1 tsp fresh ginger, minced
- 1 tbsp sesame oil (optional)

Instructions:

1. Heat vegetable oil in a wok or large skillet over medium-high heat.
2. Add garlic and ginger and cook for 30 seconds until fragrant.
3. Add the mixed vegetables and stir-fry for 5-7 minutes, until tender-crisp.
4. Stir in soy sauce, oyster sauce (if using), and sesame oil. Cook for an additional 2 minutes.
5. Serve hot as a side dish.

Caesar Salad

Ingredients:

- 4 cups romaine lettuce, chopped
- 1/4 cup grated Parmesan cheese
- 1/2 cup croutons
- 1/4 cup Caesar dressing (store-bought or homemade)

Instructions:

1. In a large bowl, toss the lettuce with the Caesar dressing.
2. Sprinkle with Parmesan cheese and croutons.
3. Serve immediately as a side dish.

Roasted Garlic

Ingredients:

- 1 head garlic
- 1 tbsp olive oil
- Salt & pepper

Instructions:

1. Preheat oven to 400°F (200°C).
2. Slice the top off the garlic head, exposing the cloves.
3. Drizzle with olive oil and sprinkle with salt and pepper.
4. Wrap the garlic in aluminum foil and roast for 35-40 minutes, until soft and golden.
5. Squeeze out the roasted garlic from the skins and use as desired.

Simple Vinaigrette

Ingredients:

- 1/4 cup olive oil
- 2 tbsp red wine vinegar (or balsamic vinegar)
- 1 tsp Dijon mustard
- Salt & pepper to taste

Instructions:

1. Whisk together the olive oil, vinegar, Dijon mustard, salt, and pepper in a small bowl.
2. Taste and adjust seasoning as needed.
3. Drizzle over your favorite salad or vegetables.

Omelette

Ingredients:

- 3 large eggs
- 2 tbsp milk or cream
- Salt & pepper, to taste
- 1 tbsp butter or oil
- Filling options: cheese, ham, mushrooms, spinach, tomatoes, etc.

Instructions:

1. In a bowl, whisk together the eggs, milk, salt, and pepper.
2. Heat butter or oil in a non-stick skillet over medium heat.
3. Pour in the egg mixture and swirl the pan to evenly distribute.
4. As the eggs begin to set, gently lift the edges and tilt the pan to let the uncooked eggs flow to the edges.
5. Once mostly set, add fillings to one half of the omelette.
6. Fold the omelette in half and cook for another minute. Serve immediately.

Baked Potatoes

Ingredients:

- 4 large russet potatoes
- Olive oil
- Salt

Instructions:

1. Preheat the oven to 400°F (200°C).
2. Scrub the potatoes and prick them with a fork a few times.
3. Rub each potato with olive oil and sprinkle with salt.
4. Place the potatoes on a baking sheet and bake for 45-60 minutes, until tender when pierced with a fork.
5. Serve with butter, sour cream, cheese, or any desired toppings.

Tomato Soup

Ingredients:

- 1 tbsp olive oil
- 1 medium onion, chopped
- 2 cloves garlic, minced
- 1 (28 oz) can crushed tomatoes
- 2 cups chicken or vegetable broth
- 1 tsp dried basil
- Salt & pepper, to taste
- 1/2 cup heavy cream (optional)

Instructions:

1. Heat olive oil in a large pot over medium heat. Add the onion and garlic, and sauté for 5 minutes until softened.
2. Add the crushed tomatoes, broth, basil, salt, and pepper. Bring to a simmer.
3. Cook for 20-30 minutes, allowing the flavors to meld.
4. Blend with an immersion blender or transfer to a blender until smooth.
5. Stir in heavy cream if desired and serve hot.

Chicken Salad

Ingredients:

- 2 cups cooked, shredded chicken
- 1/2 cup mayonnaise
- 1 tbsp Dijon mustard
- 1 tbsp lemon juice
- Salt & pepper to taste
- 1/4 cup chopped celery
- 1/4 cup chopped red onion
- Optional: grapes, almonds, or other add-ins

Instructions:

1. In a large bowl, combine shredded chicken, mayonnaise, mustard, lemon juice, salt, and pepper.
2. Stir in the chopped celery and onion.
3. Add any optional ingredients, such as grapes or almonds, for extra flavor and texture.
4. Serve on a bed of greens, in a sandwich, or with crackers.

Basic Risotto

Ingredients:

- 1 tbsp olive oil or butter
- 1 small onion, chopped
- 1 cup Arborio rice
- 4 cups chicken or vegetable broth, warmed
- 1/2 cup white wine (optional)
- 1/2 cup grated Parmesan cheese
- Salt & pepper to taste

Instructions:

1. Heat olive oil or butter in a large saucepan over medium heat.
2. Add the onion and cook for 2-3 minutes until softened.
3. Stir in the Arborio rice and cook for 1-2 minutes, allowing the rice to lightly toast.
4. Add the white wine (if using) and cook until absorbed.
5. Add the warmed broth one ladle at a time, stirring constantly and letting each addition absorb before adding more.
6. Continue adding broth and stirring for about 18-20 minutes until the rice is tender and creamy.
7. Stir in the Parmesan cheese and season with salt and pepper. Serve immediately.

Sautéed Shrimp

Ingredients:

- 1 lb large shrimp, peeled and deveined
- 2 tbsp olive oil or butter
- 3 cloves garlic, minced
- Salt & pepper to taste
- 1 tbsp lemon juice
- 1 tbsp fresh parsley, chopped (optional)

Instructions:

1. Heat olive oil or butter in a large skillet over medium-high heat.
2. Add the shrimp and season with salt and pepper.
3. Sauté the shrimp for 2-3 minutes on each side, until they turn pink and opaque.
4. Add garlic and cook for 30 seconds until fragrant.
5. Stir in lemon juice and parsley.
6. Serve immediately with rice, pasta, or as an appetizer.

Simple Beef Stir-Fry

Ingredients:

- 1 lb beef (sirloin or flank steak), thinly sliced
- 2 tbsp soy sauce
- 1 tbsp hoisin sauce
- 1 tbsp sesame oil
- 1 tbsp vegetable oil
- 1 onion, sliced
- 2 bell peppers, sliced
- 2 cloves garlic, minced
- 1/2 cup snow peas
- 1/4 cup beef broth or water
- Salt & pepper to taste

Instructions:

1. In a bowl, combine soy sauce, hoisin sauce, sesame oil, and beef broth.
2. Heat vegetable oil in a large skillet over medium-high heat.
3. Add beef and cook until browned, about 3-4 minutes. Remove and set aside.
4. In the same skillet, add onion, bell peppers, and snow peas. Cook for 3-4 minutes until softened.
5. Add garlic and cook for 30 seconds.

6. Return the beef to the pan and add the sauce mixture. Cook for an additional 2-3 minutes, until heated through.

7. Serve over rice or noodles.

Roasted Chicken

Ingredients:

- 1 whole chicken (about 4-5 lbs)
- 2 tbsp olive oil
- 1 lemon, halved
- 1 onion, quartered
- 4 cloves garlic, smashed
- Fresh rosemary or thyme sprigs
- Salt & pepper to taste

Instructions:

1. Preheat oven to 425°F (220°C).
2. Pat the chicken dry with paper towels and place it on a roasting pan.
3. Drizzle olive oil over the chicken and season generously with salt and pepper.
4. Stuff the chicken cavity with lemon halves, onion, garlic, and herbs.
5. Roast the chicken for 1 hour 20 minutes, or until the internal temperature reaches 165°F (74°C).
6. Let the chicken rest for 10 minutes before carving.

Creamed Spinach

Ingredients:

- 1 lb fresh spinach (or 2 cups frozen spinach)
- 2 tbsp butter
- 1/2 cup heavy cream
- 1/4 tsp nutmeg
- Salt & pepper to taste
- 1/2 cup grated Parmesan cheese

Instructions:

1. If using fresh spinach, wilt it in a large skillet with a little water. Drain and squeeze out excess liquid. If using frozen spinach, thaw and drain it.
2. In a large skillet, melt butter over medium heat. Add spinach and sauté for 1-2 minutes.
3. Add heavy cream, nutmeg, salt, and pepper. Stir and cook for 3-4 minutes, until the mixture thickens.
4. Stir in Parmesan cheese and cook for an additional minute.
5. Serve as a side dish.

Perfectly Cooked Quinoa

Ingredients:

- 1 cup quinoa
- 2 cups water or broth
- Salt to taste

Instructions:

1. Rinse quinoa under cold water to remove the saponin (the bitter coating).
2. Combine quinoa and water (or broth) in a medium saucepan.
3. Bring to a boil, then reduce heat to low, cover, and simmer for 15 minutes.
4. Remove from heat and let it sit, covered, for 5 minutes.
5. Fluff with a fork and season with salt.

Garlic Butter Sauce

Ingredients:

- 4 tbsp butter
- 3 cloves garlic, minced
- 1 tbsp fresh parsley, chopped
- Salt & pepper to taste
- 1 tsp lemon juice (optional)

Instructions:

1. In a small saucepan, melt butter over medium heat.
2. Add garlic and cook for 1-2 minutes until fragrant.
3. Stir in parsley, salt, and pepper.
4. If desired, add lemon juice for extra freshness.
5. Serve over seafood, pasta, or roasted vegetables.

Homemade Granola

Ingredients:

- 3 cups rolled oats
- 1/2 cup honey or maple syrup
- 1/4 cup coconut oil or olive oil
- 1/2 cup nuts (almonds, walnuts, etc.)
- 1/2 cup dried fruit (raisins, cranberries, etc.)
- 1/2 tsp vanilla extract
- 1/2 tsp cinnamon
- Pinch of salt

Instructions:

1. Preheat oven to 350°F (175°C).
2. In a large bowl, combine oats, nuts, cinnamon, and salt.
3. In a small saucepan, melt coconut oil and honey (or maple syrup). Stir in vanilla extract.
4. Pour the wet mixture over the dry ingredients and mix until coated.
5. Spread the mixture in an even layer on a baking sheet.
6. Bake for 20-25 minutes, stirring halfway through, until golden brown.
7. Remove from the oven and let cool. Stir in dried fruit before serving.

Potato Salad

Ingredients:

- 2 lbs potatoes, peeled and cubed
- 1 cup mayonnaise
- 1 tbsp Dijon mustard
- 1 tbsp white vinegar
- 1/2 cup celery, chopped
- 1/4 cup red onion, finely chopped
- 1/4 cup pickles, chopped
- Salt & pepper to taste

Instructions:

1. Bring a large pot of salted water to a boil. Add potatoes and cook for 10-15 minutes, until tender.
2. Drain and let the potatoes cool slightly.
3. In a large bowl, combine mayonnaise, mustard, vinegar, celery, onion, pickles, salt, and pepper.
4. Add the cooled potatoes and stir to coat.
5. Chill in the fridge for at least 1 hour before serving.

Grilled Chicken Thighs

Ingredients:

- 4 bone-in, skin-on chicken thighs
- 2 tbsp olive oil
- 1 tbsp lemon juice
- 2 cloves garlic, minced
- 1 tsp paprika
- Salt & pepper to taste

Instructions:

1. Preheat the grill to medium-high heat.
2. In a small bowl, mix olive oil, lemon juice, garlic, paprika, salt, and pepper.
3. Rub the mixture over the chicken thighs.
4. Grill the chicken for 6-8 minutes per side, until the internal temperature reaches 165°F (74°C).
5. Let the chicken rest for a few minutes before serving.

Roasted Sweet Potatoes

Ingredients:

- 4 medium sweet potatoes, peeled and cubed
- 2 tbsp olive oil
- 1 tsp cinnamon
- Salt & pepper to taste

Instructions:

1. Preheat oven to 400°F (200°C).
2. Toss sweet potatoes in olive oil, cinnamon, salt, and pepper.
3. Spread them in a single layer on a baking sheet.
4. Roast for 25-30 minutes, flipping halfway through, until tender and lightly browned.
5. Serve as a side dish.

Tofu Stir-Fry

Ingredients:

- 1 block firm tofu, drained and cubed
- 2 tbsp soy sauce
- 1 tbsp sesame oil
- 1 tbsp vegetable oil
- 1 onion, sliced
- 2 bell peppers, sliced
- 2 cloves garlic, minced
- 1/2 cup snap peas
- 1 tbsp rice vinegar

Instructions:

1. Press the tofu to remove excess moisture and cut into cubes.
2. Heat vegetable oil in a large skillet or wok over medium-high heat.
3. Add tofu and cook for 5-6 minutes until golden brown on all sides. Remove from the skillet.
4. In the same skillet, add sesame oil, onion, bell peppers, and snap peas. Cook for 3-4 minutes.
5. Add garlic and cook for another 30 seconds.
6. Return tofu to the skillet and stir in soy sauce and rice vinegar.

7. Cook for an additional 2-3 minutes, then serve hot over rice.

Boiled Corn on the Cob

Ingredients:

- 4 ears of corn, husked
- Water
- Salt (optional)

Instructions:

1. Bring a large pot of water to a boil. Add a pinch of salt if desired.
2. Add the corn to the boiling water and cook for 8-10 minutes, or until tender.
3. Remove the corn with tongs and let it cool slightly.
4. Serve with butter, salt, and pepper if desired.

Classic Beef Burger

Ingredients:

- 1 lb ground beef (80% lean)
- Salt and pepper to taste
- 4 burger buns
- Optional toppings: lettuce, tomato, onion, pickles, cheese, ketchup, mustard

Instructions:

1. Divide the ground beef into 4 equal portions and shape them into patties.
2. Season both sides of the patties with salt and pepper.
3. Heat a grill or skillet over medium-high heat. Cook the patties for 4-5 minutes on each side for medium doneness.
4. Toast the buns on the grill or in a pan.
5. Assemble the burgers with your preferred toppings and serve.

Baked Salmon

Ingredients:

- 4 salmon fillets
- 2 tbsp olive oil
- Salt and pepper to taste
- 1 lemon, sliced
- 1-2 sprigs fresh dill (optional)

Instructions:

1. Preheat the oven to 400°F (200°C).
2. Place the salmon fillets on a baking sheet lined with parchment paper.
3. Drizzle with olive oil and season with salt and pepper.
4. Place lemon slices on top of the salmon and add dill if using.
5. Bake for 12-15 minutes, or until the salmon easily flakes with a fork.
6. Serve with your favorite side dishes.

Roasted Carrots

Ingredients:

- 4 large carrots, peeled and cut into sticks
- 2 tbsp olive oil
- Salt and pepper to taste
- 1 tsp dried thyme or rosemary (optional)

Instructions:

1. Preheat the oven to 400°F (200°C).
2. Toss the carrot sticks in olive oil, salt, pepper, and dried herbs if desired.
3. Spread the carrots on a baking sheet in a single layer.
4. Roast for 20-25 minutes, flipping halfway through, until tender and lightly browned.
5. Serve as a side dish.

Simple Fried Rice

Ingredients:

- 2 cups cooked rice (preferably cold)
- 2 tbsp vegetable oil
- 1/2 onion, chopped
- 2 cloves garlic, minced
- 1 cup mixed vegetables (peas, carrots, corn, etc.)
- 2 eggs, lightly beaten
- 2 tbsp soy sauce
- Salt and pepper to taste

Instructions:

1. Heat 1 tbsp of vegetable oil in a large skillet or wok over medium-high heat.
2. Add the onion and garlic, cooking for 2-3 minutes until softened.
3. Add the mixed vegetables and cook for another 2-3 minutes.
4. Push the vegetables to one side and add the remaining oil. Pour the beaten eggs into the empty side and scramble.
5. Add the cold rice and soy sauce, stirring to combine.
6. Cook for 4-5 minutes, stirring occasionally, until heated through.
7. Season with salt and pepper and serve.

Vegetable Soup

Ingredients:

- 1 tbsp olive oil
- 1 onion, chopped
- 2 carrots, sliced
- 2 celery stalks, chopped
- 2 cloves garlic, minced
- 4 cups vegetable broth
- 1 can (15 oz) diced tomatoes
- 1 cup green beans, chopped
- 1 cup peas
- 1 tsp dried thyme
- Salt and pepper to taste

Instructions:

1. Heat olive oil in a large pot over medium heat.
2. Add onion, carrots, and celery, cooking for 5-7 minutes until softened.
3. Add garlic and cook for another minute.
4. Stir in the vegetable broth, diced tomatoes, green beans, peas, and thyme.
5. Bring to a boil, then reduce to a simmer and cook for 15-20 minutes, or until vegetables are tender.

6. Season with salt and pepper and serve.

Basic Guacamole

Ingredients:

- 3 ripe avocados, peeled and pitted
- 1/2 onion, finely chopped
- 1 clove garlic, minced
- 1 lime, juiced
- 1/2 tsp salt
- 1/4 tsp black pepper
- 1/4 cup chopped cilantro (optional)
- 1 small tomato, chopped (optional)

Instructions:

1. Mash the avocados in a bowl using a fork or potato masher.
2. Stir in onion, garlic, lime juice, salt, and pepper.
3. Add cilantro and tomato if desired.
4. Mix until combined, then taste and adjust seasoning.
5. Serve with tortilla chips or as a topping for tacos.

Perfectly Cooked Risotto

Ingredients:

- 1 cup Arborio rice
- 2 tbsp olive oil
- 1 small onion, finely chopped
- 2 cloves garlic, minced
- 4 cups chicken or vegetable broth, kept warm
- 1/2 cup dry white wine (optional)
- 1/2 cup grated Parmesan cheese
- Salt and pepper to taste

Instructions:

1. In a large skillet or saucepan, heat olive oil over medium heat.
2. Add the onion and garlic, cooking for 3-4 minutes until softened.
3. Stir in the rice and cook for 1-2 minutes, allowing it to lightly toast.
4. If using wine, add it now and stir until the wine is mostly absorbed.
5. Add a ladle of warm broth to the rice, stirring continuously until the liquid is absorbed.
6. Continue adding broth, one ladle at a time, stirring often, until the rice is creamy and tender (about 18-20 minutes).
7. Stir in Parmesan cheese, and season with salt and pepper.

8. Serve immediately.

Pan-Seared Steak

Ingredients:

- 2 ribeye or sirloin steaks (1-inch thick)
- 2 tbsp olive oil
- 2 cloves garlic, smashed
- 2 sprigs fresh rosemary or thyme (optional)
- Salt and pepper to taste

Instructions:

1. Heat olive oil in a large skillet over high heat.
2. Season the steaks generously with salt and pepper.
3. Add the steaks to the hot skillet and sear for 4-5 minutes per side, until desired doneness is reached (medium-rare is typically 130°F (54°C)).
4. Add garlic and herbs to the skillet during the last minute of cooking.
5. Remove the steaks from the skillet and let them rest for 5 minutes before serving.

Crispy Roasted Chicken Wings

Ingredients:

- 10-12 chicken wings
- 2 tbsp olive oil
- 1 tsp garlic powder
- 1 tsp onion powder
- 1/2 tsp smoked paprika
- Salt and pepper to taste

Instructions:

1. Preheat the oven to 425°F (220°C).
2. Toss the chicken wings with olive oil, garlic powder, onion powder, smoked paprika, salt, and pepper.
3. Place the wings on a baking sheet lined with parchment paper, ensuring they are spaced out.
4. Roast for 35-40 minutes, flipping halfway through, until the wings are crispy and golden.
5. Serve with your favorite dipping sauce.

Cabbage Slaw

Ingredients:

- 1 small head of green cabbage, shredded
- 1 small head of purple cabbage, shredded (optional for color)
- 2 large carrots, grated
- 1/2 red onion, thinly sliced
- 1/2 cup mayonnaise
- 1 tbsp apple cider vinegar
- 1 tbsp Dijon mustard
- 1 tsp sugar
- Salt and pepper to taste

Instructions:

1. In a large bowl, combine the shredded cabbage, grated carrots, and red onion.
2. In a separate small bowl, whisk together mayonnaise, apple cider vinegar, Dijon mustard, sugar, salt, and pepper.
3. Pour the dressing over the cabbage mixture and toss to coat evenly.
4. Chill in the refrigerator for at least 30 minutes before serving to allow flavors to meld.
5. Serve chilled.

Fluffy Biscuits

Ingredients:

- 2 cups all-purpose flour
- 1 tbsp baking powder
- 1/2 tsp salt
- 6 tbsp cold unsalted butter, cubed
- 3/4 cup buttermilk (or regular milk if unavailable)
- 1 tbsp melted butter (for brushing)

Instructions:

1. Preheat the oven to 450°F (230°C).
2. In a large bowl, combine flour, baking powder, and salt.
3. Add the cubed butter and use a pastry cutter or your fingers to work the butter into the flour until it resembles coarse crumbs.
4. Make a well in the center and pour in the buttermilk. Stir gently with a spoon until just combined.
5. Turn the dough out onto a lightly floured surface and gently knead 4-5 times until it comes together.
6. Pat the dough into a 1-inch thick rectangle and use a biscuit cutter to cut out biscuits.
7. Place the biscuits on a baking sheet and bake for 12-15 minutes or until golden brown.
8. Brush with melted butter and serve warm.

Homemade Croutons

Ingredients:

- 4 slices of day-old bread (French or sourdough works well)
- 2 tbsp olive oil
- 1/2 tsp garlic powder
- 1/2 tsp dried oregano
- Salt and pepper to taste

Instructions:

1. Preheat your oven to 375°F (190°C).
2. Cut the bread into small cubes.
3. In a large bowl, toss the bread cubes with olive oil, garlic powder, oregano, salt, and pepper.
4. Spread the bread cubes in a single layer on a baking sheet.
5. Bake for 10-15 minutes, stirring halfway through, until the croutons are golden and crispy.
6. Let cool and use to garnish soups or salads.

Simple Tomato Sauce

Ingredients:

- 2 tbsp olive oil
- 1 small onion, finely chopped
- 2 cloves garlic, minced
- 1 can (28 oz) crushed tomatoes
- 1 tsp dried basil
- 1 tsp dried oregano
- Salt and pepper to taste
- 1 tbsp sugar (optional, to cut acidity)

Instructions:

1. Heat olive oil in a large saucepan over medium heat. Add onion and cook for 3-4 minutes until softened.
2. Add garlic and cook for another minute, stirring to prevent burning.
3. Pour in the crushed tomatoes, basil, oregano, salt, and pepper. Stir to combine.
4. Simmer on low heat for 20-30 minutes, stirring occasionally.
5. Taste and add sugar if you prefer a sweeter sauce to balance the acidity.
6. Use the sauce for pasta, pizza, or any dish requiring tomato sauce.

Grilled Vegetables

Ingredients:

- 1 zucchini, sliced into rounds
- 1 bell pepper, cut into strips
- 1 red onion, cut into wedges
- 1 cup cherry tomatoes
- 2 tbsp olive oil
- 1 tbsp balsamic vinegar (optional)
- Salt and pepper to taste
- Fresh herbs (like rosemary or thyme), optional

Instructions:

1. Preheat the grill to medium heat.
2. Toss the vegetables in olive oil, balsamic vinegar, salt, pepper, and any fresh herbs you like.
3. Place the vegetables on the grill and cook for 5-7 minutes, turning occasionally, until tender and lightly charred.
4. Remove from the grill and serve warm as a side dish.

Baked Mac and Cheese

Ingredients:

- 1 lb elbow macaroni
- 2 tbsp butter
- 2 tbsp all-purpose flour
- 2 cups milk
- 2 cups shredded sharp cheddar cheese
- 1/2 cup grated Parmesan cheese
- 1 tsp mustard powder
- Salt and pepper to taste
- 1/2 cup breadcrumbs (for topping)

Instructions:

1. Preheat the oven to 350°F (175°C).
2. Cook the macaroni according to package instructions. Drain and set aside.
3. In a large saucepan, melt butter over medium heat. Add flour and whisk to form a roux.
4. Gradually whisk in milk and cook until the sauce thickens, about 5 minutes.
5. Stir in the cheddar and Parmesan cheese, mustard powder, salt, and pepper. Remove from heat and mix with the cooked macaroni.
6. Transfer the mac and cheese to a baking dish and sprinkle breadcrumbs on top.

7. Bake for 20 minutes, or until the top is golden and bubbly. Serve hot.

Classic Meatloaf

Ingredients:

- 1 lb ground beef
- 1/2 lb ground pork
- 1 small onion, finely chopped
- 2 cloves garlic, minced
- 1 egg
- 1/2 cup breadcrumbs
- 1/4 cup milk
- 1 tbsp Worcestershire sauce
- 1 tbsp ketchup
- Salt and pepper to taste
- 1/4 cup ketchup (for topping)

Instructions:

1. Preheat the oven to 375°F (190°C).
2. In a large bowl, combine ground beef, ground pork, onion, garlic, egg, breadcrumbs, milk, Worcestershire sauce, ketchup, salt, and pepper.
3. Mix until just combined. Do not overmix.
4. Form the mixture into a loaf shape and place it in a greased baking dish.
5. Spread 1/4 cup ketchup over the top of the meatloaf.

6. Bake for 45-55 minutes, or until cooked through (internal temperature should be 160°F or 71°C).

7. Let the meatloaf rest for 10 minutes before slicing and serving.

www.ingramcontent.com/pod-product-compliance
Lightning Source LLC
LaVergne TN
LVHW081319060526
838201LV00055B/2373